THE
SELF-CARE
JOURNAL
for TEENS

This Journal
belongs to:

START DATE: _____

The Self-Care Journal
FOR TEENS

Build a life-changing practice of self-care with this guided workbook!

As a teen or young adult, you are learning to care for the most important person in the world – yourself!

This journal gives you the tools **to observe how you spend your time and to reflect on what you appreciate the most** and makes you happy.

It includes **60-day habit tracker pages and space for daily, bedtime, reflections.** By observing your current habits and reflecting on your days with intention and dedication, you can regularly make decisions in order to take better care of yourself and be happier.

Get started on this **60-day challenge to improve your life** by integrating self-care and positive inspiration.

The Self-Care Journal
FOR TEENS

— MY BUCKET LIST —

- [ ] Go camping
- [ ] Have a water fight
- [ ] Make homemade pizza
- [ ] Try a new hairstyle
- [ ] Redecorate my room
- [ ] Visit a different country
- [ ] Go fishing
- [ ] Plant a tree
- [ ] Complete a puzzle
- [ ] Go on a bike ride
- [ ] Hike a new trail
- [ ] Earn some money
- [ ] Collect shells
- [ ] Visit a waterfall
- [ ] Build a snowman
- [ ] Go to a concert/theatre
- [ ] Make homemade ice cream
- [ ] Write a story
- [ ] Go to the zoo
- [ ] Dance in the rain
- [ ] Run in a race
- [ ] Have a bowling night
- [ ] Play mini golf
- [ ] Go to the beach/lake
- [ ] Have a picnic with friends
- [ ] Stay up all night
- [ ] Do some volunteering

_____
_____
_____
_____
_____
_____
_____
_____
_____
_____
_____
_____
_____
_____
_____
_____
_____
_____
_____
_____
_____
_____
_____
_____
_____
_____

The Self-Care Journal
FOR TEENS

— MY WISH LIST —

Series and Movies to Watch

Books to Read

The Self-Care Journal
FOR TEENS

DAY 1

DATE: _____   Mo Tu We Th Fr Sa Su

— HABIT TRACKER —

Daily Basics

- SLEEP LOG | Duration: _____ Times: From _____ To _____
- CUPS OF WATER: _____
- HEALTHY EATING: Yes ☐   No ☐
- TIME OUTSIDE: _____

Mind

	Duration
○ Study	
○ Reading	
○ Phone/Social Media	
○ TV/Series	
○ Listening to Music	
○ Creative Work	
○ Other: _____	
○ Other: _____	
○ Other: _____	

Body

	Type	Duration
	Example: 15 push-ups	
● Exercise		

- ● Shower: Yes ☐   No ☐
- ● Hair Wash: Yes ☐   No ☐
- ● Skincare Routine: Yes ☐   No ☐

Mood Tracker

Today I have felt...

😃 🙂 😐 🙁 😣
☐   ☐   ☐   ☐   ☐

The Self-Care Journal
FOR TEENS

REFLECTION

Gratitude

- Today I am grateful for _____

_____

_____

_____

- Best moments of the day:

_____

_____

_____

My notes/My thoughts

A POSITIVE AFFIRMATION

The Self-Care Journal
FOR TEENS

DAY 2

DATE: _____   Mo Tu We Th Fr Sa Su

— HABIT TRACKER —

Daily Basics

- SLEEP LOG | Duration: _____ Times: From _____ To _____
- CUPS OF WATER: _____
- HEALTHY EATING: Yes ☐   No ☐
- TIME OUTSIDE: _____

Mind

	Duration
Study	
Reading	
Phone/Social Media	
TV/Series	
Listening to Music	
Creative Work	
Other: _____	
Other: _____	
Other: _____	

Body

	Type *Example: 15 push-ups*	Duration
Exercise		

- Shower: Yes ☐ No ☐
- Hair Wash: Yes ☐ No ☐
- Skincare Routine: Yes ☐ No ☐

Mood Tracker

Today I have felt...

☐ ☐ ☐ ☐ ☐

The Self-Care Journal
FOR TEENS

— REFLECTION —

✿ Gratitude

- Today I am grateful for _____

_____

_____

_____

- Best moments of the day:

_____

_____

_____

My notes/My thoughts

A POSITIVE AFFIRMATION

The Self-Care Journal
FOR TEENS

DAY 3

DATE: _____   Mo Tu We Th Fr Sa Su

— HABIT TRACKER —

Daily Basics

- SLEEP LOG | Duration: _____ Times: From _____ To _____
- CUPS OF WATER: _____
- HEALTHY EATING: Yes ☐   No ☐
- TIME OUTSIDE: _____

Mind

	Duration
○ Study	
○ Reading	
○ Phone/Social Media	
○ TV/Series	
○ Listening to Music	
○ Creative Work	
○ Other: _____	
○ Other: _____	
○ Other: _____	

Body

	Type _Example: 15 push-ups_	Duration
● Exercise		

- ● Shower: Yes ☐   No ☐
- ● Hair Wash: Yes ☐   No ☐
- ● Skincare Routine: Yes ☐   No ☐

Mood Tracker

Today I have felt...

☐   ☐   ☐   ☐   ☐

The Self-Care Journal
FOR TEENS

REFLECTION

Gratitude

- Today I am grateful for _____

_____

_____

_____

- Best moments of the day:

_____

_____

_____

My notes/My thoughts

A POSITIVE AFFIRMATION

The Self-Care Journal
FOR TEENS

DAY 4

DATE: _____   Mo Tu We Th Fr Sa Su

— HABIT TRACKER —

Daily Basics

- SLEEP LOG | Duration: _____ Times: From _____ To _____
- CUPS OF WATER: _____
- HEALTHY EATING: Yes ☐   No ☐
- TIME OUTSIDE: _____

Mind

	Duration
Study	
Reading	
Phone/Social Media	
TV/Series	
Listening to Music	
Creative Work	
Other: _____	
Other: _____	
Other: _____	

Body

	Type *Example: 15 push-ups*	Duration
Exercise		

- Shower: Yes ☐   No ☐
- Hair Wash: Yes ☐   No ☐
- Skincare Routine: Yes ☐   No ☐

Mood Tracker

Today I have felt...

☐   ☐   ☐   ☐   ☐

The Self-Care Journal
FOR TEENS

REFLECTION

Gratitude

- Today I am grateful for _____

_____

_____

_____

- Best moments of the day:

_____

_____

_____

My notes/My thoughts

A POSITIVE AFFIRMATION

The Self-Care Journal
FOR TEENS

DAY 5

DATE: _____   Mo Tu We Th Fr Sa Su

— HABIT TRACKER —

Daily Basics

- SLEEP LOG | Duration: _____ Times: From _____ To _____
- CUPS OF WATER: _____
- HEALTHY EATING: Yes ☐   No ☐
- TIME OUTSIDE: _____

Mind

	Duration
Study	
Reading	
Phone/Social Media	
TV/Series	
Listening to Music	
Creative Work	
Other: _____	
Other: _____	
Other: _____	

Body

	Type	Duration
	Example: 15 push-ups	
Exercise		

- Shower: Yes ☐ No ☐
- Hair Wash: Yes ☐ No ☐
- Skincare Routine: Yes ☐ No ☐

Mood Tracker

Today I have felt...

☐ ☐ ☐ ☐ ☐

The Self-Care Journal
FOR TEENS

REFLECTION

Gratitude

- Today I am grateful for _____

_____

_____

_____

- Best moments of the day:

_____

_____

_____

My notes/My thoughts

A POSITIVE AFFIRMATION

The Self-Care Journal
FOR TEENS

DAY 6

DATE: _____ Mo Tu We Th Fr Sa Su

— HABIT TRACKER —

Daily Basics

- SLEEP LOG | Duration: _____ Times: From _____ To _____
- CUPS OF WATER: _____
- HEALTHY EATING: Yes ☐   No ☐
- TIME OUTSIDE: _____

Mind

	Duration
Study	
Reading	
Phone/Social Media	
TV/Series	
Listening to Music	
Creative Work	
Other: _____	
Other: _____	
Other: _____	

Body

	Type Example: 15 push-ups	Duration
Exercise		

- Shower: Yes ☐   No ☐
- Hair Wash: Yes ☐   No ☐
- Skincare Routine: Yes ☐   No ☐

Mood Tracker

Today I have felt...

☐ ☐ ☐ ☐ ☐

The Self-Care Journal
FOR TEENS

— REFLECTION —

🌸 Gratitude

● Today I am grateful for _____

_____

_____

_____

● Best moments of the day:

_____

_____

_____

My notes/My thoughts

A POSITIVE AFFIRMATION

The Self-Care Journal
FOR TEENS

DAY 7

DATE: _____   Mo Tu We Th Fr Sa Su

— HABIT TRACKER —

Daily Basics

- SLEEP LOG | Duration: _____ Times: From _____ To _____
- CUPS OF WATER: _____
- HEALTHY EATING: Yes ☐   No ☐
- TIME OUTSIDE: _____

Mind

	Duration
Study	
Reading	
Phone/Social Media	
TV/Series	
Listening to Music	
Creative Work	
Other: _____	
Other: _____	
Other: _____	

Body

	Type _Example: 15 push-ups_	Duration
Exercise		

- Shower: Yes ☐   No ☐
- Hair Wash: Yes ☐   No ☐
- Skincare Routine: Yes ☐   No ☐

Mood Tracker

Today I have felt...

☐   ☐   ☐   ☐   ☐

The Self-Care Journal
FOR TEENS

— REFLECTION —

Gratitude

● Today I am grateful for _____

_____

_____

_____

● Best moments of the day:

_____

_____

_____

My notes/My thoughts

A POSITIVE AFFIRMATION

The Self-Care Journal
FOR TEENS

DAY 8

DATE: _____   Mo Tu We Th Fr Sa Su

— HABIT TRACKER —

Daily Basics

- SLEEP LOG | Duration: _____ Times: From _____ To _____
- CUPS OF WATER: _____
- HEALTHY EATING: Yes ☐   No ☐
- TIME OUTSIDE: _____

Mind

	Duration
Study	
Reading	
Phone/Social Media	
TV/Series	
Listening to Music	
Creative Work	
Other: _____	
Other: _____	
Other: _____	

Body

	Type Example: 15 push-ups	Duration
Exercise		

- Shower: Yes ☐   No ☐
- Hair Wash: Yes ☐   No ☐
- Skincare Routine: Yes ☐   No ☐

Mood Tracker

Today I have felt...

☐ ☐ ☐ ☐ ☐

The Self-Care Journal
FOR TEENS

REFLECTION

Gratitude

- Today I am grateful for _____

_____

_____

_____

- Best moments of the day:

_____

_____

_____

My notes/My thoughts

A POSITIVE AFFIRMATION

The Self-Care Journal
FOR TEENS

DAY 9

DATE: _____   Mo Tu We Th Fr Sa Su

— HABIT TRACKER —

Daily Basics

- SLEEP LOG | Duration: _____ Times: From _____ To _____
- CUPS OF WATER: _____
- HEALTHY EATING: Yes ☐   No ☐
- TIME OUTSIDE: _____

Mind

	Duration
○ Study	
○ Reading	
○ Phone/Social Media	
○ TV/Series	
○ Listening to Music	
○ Creative Work	
○ Other: _____	
○ Other: _____	
○ Other: _____	

Body

	Type	Duration
● Exercise	*Example: 15 push-ups*	

- Shower: Yes ☐ No ☐
- Hair Wash: Yes ☐ No ☐
- Skincare Routine: Yes ☐   No ☐

Mood Tracker

Today I have felt...

😀 🙂 😐 🙁 😡

☐   ☐   ☐   ☐   ☐

The Self-Care Journal
FOR TEENS

REFLECTION

🌸 Gratitude

● Today I am grateful for _____

_____

_____

_____

● Best moments of the day:

_____

_____

_____

My notes/My thoughts

A POSITIVE AFFIRMATION

The Self-Care Journal
FOR TEENS

DAY 10

DATE: _____   Mo Tu We Th Fr Sa Su

— HABIT TRACKER —

✿ Daily Basics

- SLEEP LOG | Duration: _____ Times: From _____ To _____
- CUPS OF WATER: _____
- HEALTHY EATING: Yes ☐   No ☐
- TIME OUTSIDE: _____

Mind

	Duration
Study	
Reading	
Phone/Social Media	
TV/Series	
Listening to Music	
Creative Work	
Other: _____	
Other: _____	
Other: _____	

Body

	Type	Duration
	Example: 15 push-ups	
Exercise		

- Shower: Yes ☐   No ☐
- Hair Wash: Yes ☐   No ☐
- Skincare Routine: Yes ☐   No ☐

Mood Tracker

Today I have felt...

😀 🙂 😐 🙁 😠
☐ ☐ ☐ ☐ ☐

The Self-Care Journal
FOR TEENS

REFLECTION

❋ Gratitude

● Today I am grateful for _____

_____

_____

_____

● Best moments of the day:

_____

_____

_____

My notes/My thoughts

A POSITIVE AFFIRMATION

The Self-Care Journal
FOR TEENS

DAY 11

DATE: _____   Mo Tu We Th Fr Sa Su

— HABIT TRACKER —

Daily Basics

- SLEEP LOG | Duration: _____ Times: From _____ To _____
- CUPS OF WATER: _____
- HEALTHY EATING: Yes ☐   No ☐
- TIME OUTSIDE: _____

Mind

	Duration
Study	
Reading	
Phone/Social Media	
TV/Series	
Listening to Music	
Creative Work	
Other: _____	
Other: _____	
Other: _____	

Body

	Type	Duration
Exercise	*Example: 15 push-ups*	

- Shower: Yes ☐   No ☐
- Hair Wash: Yes ☐   No ☐
- Skincare Routine: Yes ☐   No ☐

Mood Tracker

Today I have felt...

☐ ☐ ☐ ☐ ☐

REFLECTION

✿ Gratitude

- Today I am grateful for _____

_____

_____

_____

- Best moments of the day:

_____

_____

_____

My notes/My thoughts

.

A POSITIVE AFFIRMATION

The Self-Care Journal
FOR TEENS

DAY 12

DATE: _____   Mo Tu We Th Fr Sa Su

— HABIT TRACKER —

Daily Basics

- SLEEP LOG | Duration: _____ Times: From _____ To _____
- CUPS OF WATER: _____
- HEALTHY EATING: Yes ☐   No ☐
- TIME OUTSIDE: _____

Mind

	Duration
Study	
Reading	
Phone/Social Media	
TV/Series	
Listening to Music	
Creative Work	
Other: _____	
Other: _____	
Other: _____	

Body

	Type Example: 15 push-ups	Duration
Exercise		

- Shower: Yes ☐ No ☐
- Hair Wash: Yes ☐ No ☐
- Skincare Routine: Yes ☐   No ☐

Mood Tracker

Today I have felt...

☐ ☐ ☐ ☐ ☐

The Self-Care Journal
FOR TEENS

REFLECTION

Gratitude

- Today I am grateful for _____

_____

_____

_____

- Best moments of the day:

_____

_____

_____

My notes/My thoughts

A POSITIVE AFFIRMATION

The Self-Care Journal
FOR TEENS

DAY 13

DATE: _____   Mo Tu We Th Fr Sa Su

— HABIT TRACKER —

Daily Basics

- SLEEP LOG | Duration: _____ Times: From _____ To _____
- CUPS OF WATER: _____
- HEALTHY EATING: Yes ☐   No ☐
- TIME OUTSIDE: _____

Mind

	Duration
○ Study	
○ Reading	
○ Phone/Social Media	
○ TV/Series	
○ Listening to Music	
○ Creative Work	
○ Other: _____	
○ Other: _____	
○ Other: _____	

Body

	Type *Example: 15 push-ups*	Duration
● Exercise		

- ● Shower: Yes ☐   No ☐
- ● Hair Wash: Yes ☐   No ☐
- ● Skincare Routine: Yes ☐   No ☐

Mood Tracker

Today I have felt...

☐   ☐   ☐   ☐   ☐

The Self-Care Journal
FOR TEENS

REFLECTION

Gratitude

● Today I am grateful for _____

_____

_____

_____

● Best moments of the day:

_____

_____

_____

My notes/My thoughts

A POSITIVE AFFIRMATION

The Self-Care Journal
FOR TEENS

DAY 14

DATE: _____   Mo Tu We Th Fr Sa Su

— HABIT TRACKER —

✿ Daily Basics

- SLEEP LOG | Duration: _____ Times: From _____ To _____
- CUPS OF WATER: _____
- HEALTHY EATING: Yes ☐   No ☐
- TIME OUTSIDE: _____

Mind

	Duration
○ Study	
○ Reading	
○ Phone/Social Media	
○ TV/Series	
○ Listening to Music	
○ Creative Work	
○ Other: _____	
○ Other: _____	
○ Other: _____	

Body

	Type *Example: 15 push-ups*	Duration
● Exercise		

- ● Shower: Yes ☐ No ☐
- ● Hair Wash: Yes ☐ No ☐
- ● Skincare Routine: Yes ☐ No ☐

Mood Tracker

Today I have felt...

☐ ☐ ☐ ☐ ☐

The Self-Care Journal
FOR TEENS

REFLECTION

Gratitude

- Today I am grateful for _____

_____

_____

_____

- Best moments of the day:

_____

_____

_____

My notes/My thoughts

A POSITIVE AFFIRMATION

The Self-Care Journal
FOR TEENS

DAY 15

DATE: _____   Mo Tu We Th Fr Sa Su

— HABIT TRACKER —

Daily Basics

- SLEEP LOG | Duration: _____ Times: From _____ To _____
- CUPS OF WATER: _____
- HEALTHY EATING: Yes ☐   No ☐
- TIME OUTSIDE: _____

Mind

	Duration
Study	
Reading	
Phone/Social Media	
TV/Series	
Listening to Music	
Creative Work	
Other: _____	
Other: _____	
Other: _____	

Body

	Type *Example: 15 push-ups*	Duration
Exercise		

- Shower: Yes ☐ No ☐
- Hair Wash: Yes ☐ No ☐
- Skincare Routine: Yes ☐ No ☐

Mood Tracker

Today I have felt...

☐ ☐ ☐ ☐ ☐

The Self-Care Journal
FOR TEENS

DAY 15

Gratitude

- Today I am grateful for _____

_____

_____

_____

- Best moments of the day:

_____

_____

_____

My notes/My thoughts

A POSITIVE AFFIRMATION

The Self-Care Journal
FOR TEENS

DAY 16

DATE: _____   Mo Tu We Th Fr Sa Su

— HABIT TRACKER —

✿ Daily Basics

- SLEEP LOG | Duration: _____ Times: From _____ To _____
- CUPS OF WATER: _____
- HEALTHY EATING: Yes ☐   No ☐
- TIME OUTSIDE: _____

Mind

	Duration
○ Study	
○ Reading	
○ Phone/Social Media	
○ TV/Series	
○ Listening to Music	
○ Creative Work	
○ Other: _____	
○ Other: _____	
○ Other: _____	

Body

	Type *Example: 15 push-ups*	Duration
● Exercise		

- ● Shower: Yes ☐ No ☐
- ● Hair Wash: Yes ☐   No ☐
- ● Skincare Routine: Yes ☐   No ☐

Mood Tracker

Today I have felt...

☐   ☐   ☐   ☐   ☐

The Self-Care Journal
FOR TEENS

REFLECTION

✿ Gratitude

● Today I am grateful for _____

_____

_____

_____

● Best moments of the day:

_____

_____

_____

My notes/My thoughts

A POSITIVE AFFIRMATION

The Self-Care Journal
FOR TEENS

DAY 17

DATE: _____   Mo Tu We Th Fr Sa Su

— HABIT TRACKER —

Daily Basics

- SLEEP LOG | Duration: _____ Times: From _____ To _____
- CUPS OF WATER: _____
- HEALTHY EATING: Yes ☐   No ☐
- TIME OUTSIDE: _____

Mind

	Duration
Study	
Reading	
Phone/Social Media	
TV/Series	
Listening to Music	
Creative Work	
Other: _____	
Other: _____	
Other: _____	

Body

	Type	Duration
	Example: 15 push-ups	
Exercise		

- Shower: Yes ☐ No ☐
- Hair Wash: Yes ☐ No ☐
- Skincare Routine: Yes ☐ No ☐

Mood Tracker

Today I have felt...

☐ ☐ ☐ ☐ ☐

The Self-Care Journal
FOR TEENS

REFLECTION

Gratitude

- Today I am grateful for _____

_____

_____

_____

- Best moments of the day:

_____

_____

_____

My notes/My thoughts

A POSITIVE AFFIRMATION

The Self-Care Journal
FOR TEENS

DAY 18

DATE: _____ Mo Tu We Th Fr Sa Su

— HABIT TRACKER —

Daily Basics

- SLEEP LOG | Duration: _____ Times: From _____ To _____
- CUPS OF WATER: _____
- HEALTHY EATING: Yes ☐   No ☐
- TIME OUTSIDE: _____

Mind

	Duration
Study	
Reading	
Phone/Social Media	
TV/Series	
Listening to Music	
Creative Work	
Other: _____	
Other: _____	
Other: _____	

Body

	Type	Duration
	Example: 15 push-ups	
Exercise		

- Shower: Yes ☐   No ☐
- Hair Wash: Yes ☐   No ☐
- Skincare Routine: Yes ☐   No ☐

Mood Tracker

Today I have felt...

☐ ☐ ☐ ☐ ☐

The Self-Care Journal
FOR TEENS

REFLECTION

❋ Gratitude

- Today I am grateful for _____

  _____

  _____

  _____

- Best moments of the day:

  _____

  _____

  _____

My notes/My thoughts

A POSITIVE AFFIRMATION

The Self-Care Journal
FOR TEENS

DAY 19

DATE: _____   Mo Tu We Th Fr Sa Su

— HABIT TRACKER —

Daily Basics

- SLEEP LOG | Duration: _____ Times: From _____ To _____
- CUPS OF WATER: _____
- HEALTHY EATING: Yes ☐   No ☐
- TIME OUTSIDE: _____

Mind

	Duration
○ Study	
○ Reading	
○ Phone/Social Media	
○ TV/Series	
○ Listening to Music	
○ Creative Work	
○ Other: _____	
○ Other: _____	
○ Other: _____	

Body

	Type _Example: 15 push-ups_	Duration
● Exercise		

- Shower: Yes ☐   No ☐
- Hair Wash: Yes ☐   No ☐
- Skincare Routine: Yes ☐   No ☐

Mood Tracker

Today I have felt...

☐   ☐   ☐   ☐   ☐

The Self-Care Journal
FOR TEENS

REFLECTION

🌸 Gratitude

● Today I am grateful for _____

_____

_____

_____

● Best moments of the day:

_____

_____

_____

My notes/My thoughts

A POSITIVE AFFIRMATION

The Self-Care Journal
FOR TEENS

DAY 20

DATE: _____   Mo Tu We Th Fr Sa Su

— HABIT TRACKER —

Daily Basics

- SLEEP LOG | Duration: _____ Times: From _____ To _____
- CUPS OF WATER: _____
- HEALTHY EATING: Yes ☐   No ☐
- TIME OUTSIDE: _____

Mind

	Duration
Study	
Reading	
Phone/Social Media	
TV/Series	
Listening to Music	
Creative Work	
Other: _____	
Other: _____	
Other: _____	

Body

	Type _Example: 15 push-ups_	Duration
Exercise		

- Shower: Yes ☐   No ☐
- Hair Wash: Yes ☐   No ☐
- Skincare Routine: Yes ☐   No ☐

Mood Tracker

Today I have felt...

☐ ☐ ☐ ☐ ☐

The Self-Care Journal
FOR TEENS

REFLECTION

Gratitude

- Today I am grateful for _____

_____

_____

_____

- Best moments of the day:

_____

_____

_____

My notes/My thoughts

A POSITIVE AFFIRMATION

The Self-Care Journal
FOR TEENS

DAY 21

DATE: _____   Mo Tu We Th Fr Sa Su

— HABIT TRACKER —

Daily Basics

- SLEEP LOG | Duration: _____ Times: From _____ To _____
- CUPS OF WATER: _____
- HEALTHY EATING: Yes ☐   No ☐
- TIME OUTSIDE: _____

Mind

	Duration
Study	
Reading	
Phone/Social Media	
TV/Series	
Listening to Music	
Creative Work	
Other: _____	
Other: _____	
Other: _____	

Body

	Type	Duration
Exercise	Example: 15 push-ups	

- Shower: Yes ☐   No ☐
- Hair Wash: Yes ☐   No ☐
- Skincare Routine: Yes ☐   No ☐

Mood Tracker

Today I have felt...

☐   ☐   ☐   ☐   ☐

The Self-Care Journal
FOR TEENS

DAY 21

REFLECTION

✿ Gratitude

- Today I am grateful for _____

_____

_____

_____

- Best moments of the day:

_____

_____

_____

My notes/My thoughts

A POSITIVE AFFIRMATION

The Self-Care Journal
FOR TEENS

DAY 22

DATE: _____   Mo Tu We Th Fr Sa Su

— HABIT TRACKER —

Daily Basics

- SLEEP LOG | Duration: _____ Times: From _____ To _____
- CUPS OF WATER: _____
- HEALTHY EATING: Yes ☐   No ☐
- TIME OUTSIDE: _____

Mind

	Duration
○ Study	
○ Reading	
○ Phone/Social Media	
○ TV/Series	
○ Listening to Music	
○ Creative Work	
○ Other: _____	
○ Other: _____	
○ Other: _____	

Body

	Type Example: 15 push-ups	Duration
● Exercise		

- ● Shower: Yes ☐   No ☐
- ● Hair Wash: Yes ☐   No ☐
- ● Skincare Routine: Yes ☐   No ☐

Mood Tracker

Today I have felt...

☐   ☐   ☐   ☐   ☐

The Self-Care Journal
FOR TEENS

REFLECTION

❋ Gratitude

- Today I am grateful for _____

_____

_____

_____

- Best moments of the day:

_____

_____

_____

My notes/My thoughts

A POSITIVE AFFIRMATION

The Self-Care Journal
FOR TEENS

DAY 23

DATE: _____ Mo Tu We Th Fr Sa Su

— HABIT TRACKER —

Daily Basics

- SLEEP LOG | Duration: _____ Times: From _____ To _____
- CUPS OF WATER: _____
- HEALTHY EATING: Yes ☐   No ☐
- TIME OUTSIDE: _____

Mind

	Duration
○ Study	
○ Reading	
Phone/Social Media	
TV/Series	
○ Listening to Music	
○ Creative Work	
○ Other: _____	
○ Other: _____	
○ Other: _____	

Body

	Type	Duration
	Example: 15 push-ups	
○ Exercise		

- Shower: Yes ☐   No ☐
- Hair Wash: Yes ☐   No ☐
- Skincare Routine: Yes ☐   No ☐

Mood Tracker

Today I have felt...

☐ ☐ ☐ ☐ ☐

The Self-Care Journal
FOR TEENS

REFLECTION

🌸 Gratitude

● Today I am grateful for _____

_____

_____

_____

● Best moments of the day:

_____

_____

_____

My notes/My thoughts

A POSITIVE AFFIRMATION

The Self-Care Journal
FOR TEENS

DAY 24

DATE: _____ Mo Tu We Th Fr Sa Su

— HABIT TRACKER —

Daily Basics

- SLEEP LOG | Duration: _____ Times: From _____ To _____
- CUPS OF WATER: _____
- HEALTHY EATING: Yes ☐   No ☐
- TIME OUTSIDE: _____

Mind

	Duration
Study	
Reading	
Phone/Social Media	
TV/Series	
Listening to Music	
Creative Work	
Other: _____	
Other: _____	
Other: _____	

Body

	Type Example: 15 push-ups	Duration
Exercise		

- Shower: Yes ☐ No ☐
- Hair Wash: Yes ☐ No ☐
- Skincare Routine: Yes ☐ No ☐

Mood Tracker

Today I have felt...

☐ ☐ ☐ ☐ ☐

The Self-Care Journal
FOR TEENS

REFLECTION

✿ Gratitude

- Today I am grateful for _____

_____

_____

_____

- Best moments of the day:

_____

_____

_____

My notes/My thoughts

A POSITIVE AFFIRMATION

The Self-Care Journal
FOR TEENS

DAY 25

DATE: _____ Mo Tu We Th Fr Sa Su

— HABIT TRACKER —

Daily Basics

- SLEEP LOG | Duration: _____ Times: From _____ To _____
- CUPS OF WATER: _____
- HEALTHY EATING: Yes ☐   No ☐
- TIME OUTSIDE: _____

Mind

	Duration
○ Study	
○ Reading	
○ Phone/Social Media	
○ TV/Series	
○ Listening to Music	
○ Creative Work	
○ Other: _____	
○ Other: _____	
○ Other: _____	

Body

	Type *Example: 15 push-ups*	Duration
● Exercise		

- Shower: Yes ☐   No ☐
- Hair Wash: Yes ☐   No ☐
- Skincare Routine: Yes ☐   No ☐

Mood Tracker

Today I have felt...

😀 🙂 😐 🙁 😣

☐   ☐   ☐   ☐   ☐

The Self-Care Journal
FOR TEENS

— REFLECTION —

🌸 Gratitude

- Today I am grateful for _____

  _____

  _____

  _____

- Best moments of the day:

  _____

  _____

  _____

My notes/My thoughts

A POSITIVE AFFIRMATION

The Self-Care Journal
FOR TEENS

DAY 26

DATE: _____   Mo Tu We Th Fr Sa Su

— HABIT TRACKER —

Daily Basics

- SLEEP LOG | Duration: _____ Times: From _____ To _____
- CUPS OF WATER: _____
- HEALTHY EATING: Yes ☐   No ☐
- TIME OUTSIDE: _____

Mind

	Duration
Study	
Reading	
Phone/Social Media	
TV/Series	
Listening to Music	
Creative Work	
Other: _____	
Other: _____	
Other: _____	

Body

	Type Example: 15 push-ups	Duration
Exercise		

- Shower: Yes ☐ No ☐
- Hair Wash: Yes ☐ No ☐
- Skincare Routine: Yes ☐ No ☐

Mood Tracker

Today I have felt...

☐ ☐ ☐ ☐ ☐

The Self-Care Journal
FOR TEENS

REFLECTION

❀ Gratitude

● Today I am grateful for _____

_____

_____

_____

● Best moments of the day:

_____

_____

_____

My notes/My thoughts

A POSITIVE AFFIRMATION

The Self-Care Journal
FOR TEENS

DAY 27

DATE: _____   Mo Tu We Th Fr Sa Su

— HABIT TRACKER —

Daily Basics

- SLEEP LOG | Duration: _____ Times: From _____ To _____
- CUPS OF WATER: _____
- HEALTHY EATING: Yes ☐   No ☐
- TIME OUTSIDE: _____

Mind

	Duration
Study	
Reading	
Phone/Social Media	
TV/Series	
Listening to Music	
Creative Work	
Other: _____	
Other: _____	
Other: _____	

Body

	Type	Duration
	Example: 15 push-ups	
Exercise		

- Shower: Yes ☐   No ☐
- Hair Wash: Yes ☐   No ☐
- Skincare Routine: Yes ☐   No ☐

Mood Tracker

Today I have felt...

☐   ☐   ☐   ☐   ☐

The Self-Care Journal
FOR TEENS

REFLECTION

Gratitude

- Today I am grateful for _____
_____
_____
_____

- Best moments of the day:
_____
_____
_____

My notes/My thoughts

A POSITIVE AFFIRMATION

The Self-Care Journal
FOR TEENS

DAY 28

DATE: _____   Mo Tu We Th Fr Sa Su

— HABIT TRACKER —

Daily Basics

- SLEEP LOG | Duration: _____ Times: From _____ To _____
- CUPS OF WATER: _____
- HEALTHY EATING: Yes ☐   No ☐
- TIME OUTSIDE: _____

Mind

	Duration
Study	
Reading	
Phone/Social Media	
TV/Series	
Listening to Music	
Creative Work	
Other: _____	
Other: _____	
Other: _____	

Body

	Type *Example: 15 push-ups*	Duration
Exercise		

- Shower: Yes ☐ No ☐
- Hair Wash: Yes ☐ No ☐
- Skincare Routine: Yes ☐ No ☐

Mood Tracker

Today I have felt...

☐ ☐ ☐ ☐ ☐

The Self-Care Journal
FOR TEENS

REFLECTION

🌸 Gratitude

● Today I am grateful for _____

_____

_____

_____

● Best moments of the day:

_____

_____

_____

My notes/My thoughts

A POSITIVE AFFIRMATION

The Self-Care Journal
FOR TEENS

DAY 29

DATE: _____   Mo Tu We Th Fr Sa Su

— HABIT TRACKER —

❁ Daily Basics

- SLEEP LOG | Duration: _____ Times: From _____ To _____
- CUPS OF WATER: _____
- HEALTHY EATING: Yes ☐   No ☐
- TIME OUTSIDE: _____

Mind

	Duration
○ Study	
○ Reading	
○ Phone/Social Media	
○ TV/Series	
○ Listening to Music	
○ Creative Work	
○ Other: _____	
○ Other: _____	
○ Other: _____	

Body

	Type *Example: 15 push-ups*	Duration
● Exercise		

- ● Shower: Yes ☐   No ☐
- ● Hair Wash: Yes ☐   No ☐
- ● Skincare Routine: Yes ☐   No ☐

Mood Tracker

Today I have felt...

☐   ☐   ☐   ☐   ☐

The Self-Care Journal
FOR TEENS

REFLECTION

❀ Gratitude

● Today I am grateful for _____

_____

_____

_____

● Best moments of the day:

_____

_____

_____

My notes / My thoughts

A POSITIVE AFFIRMATION

The Self-Care Journal
FOR TEENS

DAY 30

DATE: _____   Mo Tu We Th Fr Sa Su

— HABIT TRACKER —

Daily Basics

- SLEEP LOG | Duration: _____ Times: From _____ To _____
- CUPS OF WATER: _____
- HEALTHY EATING: Yes ☐   No ☐
- TIME OUTSIDE: _____

Mind

	Duration
Study	
Reading	
Phone/Social Media	
TV/Series	
Listening to Music	
Creative Work	
Other: _____	
Other: _____	
Other: _____	

Body

	Type *Example: 15 push-ups*	Duration
Exercise		

- Shower: Yes ☐ No ☐
- Hair Wash: Yes ☐ No ☐
- Skincare Routine: Yes ☐ No ☐

Mood Tracker

Today I have felt...

☺ 🙂 😐 🙁 😠

☐ ☐ ☐ ☐ ☐

The Self-Care Journal
FOR TEENS

REFLECTION

❋ Gratitude

- Today I am grateful for _____

_____

_____

_____

- Best moments of the day:

_____

_____

_____

My notes/My thoughts

A POSITIVE AFFIRMATION

The Self-Care Journal
FOR TEENS

DAY 31

DATE: _____   Mo Tu We Th Fr Sa Su

— HABIT TRACKER —

Daily Basics

- SLEEP LOG | Duration: _____ Times: From _____ To _____
- CUPS OF WATER: _____
- HEALTHY EATING: Yes ☐   No ☐
- TIME OUTSIDE: _____

Mind

	Duration
Study	
Reading	
Phone/Social Media	
TV/Series	
Listening to Music	
Creative Work	
Other: _____	
Other: _____	
Other: _____	

Body

	Type Example: 15 push-ups	Duration
Exercise		

- Shower: Yes ☐ No ☐
- Hair Wash: Yes ☐ No ☐
- Skincare Routine: Yes ☐ No ☐

Mood Tracker

Today I have felt...

☐ ☐ ☐ ☐ ☐

The Self-Care Journal
FOR TEENS

REFLECTION

❀ Gratitude

● Today I am grateful for _____

_____

_____

_____

● Best moments of the day:

_____

_____

_____

My notes / My thoughts

A POSITIVE AFFIRMATION

The Self-Care Journal
FOR TEENS

DAY 32

DATE: _____   Mo Tu We Th Fr Sa Su

— HABIT TRACKER —

Daily Basics

- SLEEP LOG | Duration: _____ Times: From _____ To _____
- CUPS OF WATER: _____
- HEALTHY EATING: Yes ☐   No ☐
- TIME OUTSIDE: _____

Mind

	Duration
Study	
Reading	
Phone/Social Media	
TV/Series	
Listening to Music	
Creative Work	
Other: _____	
Other: _____	
Other: _____	

Body

	Type *Example: 15 push-ups*	Duration
Exercise		

- Shower: Yes ☐ No ☐
- Hair Wash: Yes ☐ No ☐
- Skincare Routine: Yes ☐ No ☐

Mood Tracker

Today I have felt...

☐   ☐   ☐   ☐   ☐

The Self-Care Journal
FOR TEENS

DAY 32

REFLECTION

Gratitude

- Today I am grateful for _____

_____

_____

_____

- Best moments of the day:

_____

_____

_____

My notes/My thoughts

A POSITIVE AFFIRMATION

The Self-Care Journal
FOR TEENS

DAY 33

DATE: _____   Mo Tu We Th Fr Sa Su

— HABIT TRACKER —

Daily Basics

- SLEEP LOG | Duration: _____ Times: From _____ To _____
- CUPS OF WATER: _____
- HEALTHY EATING: Yes ☐   No ☐
- TIME OUTSIDE: _____

Mind

	Duration
Study	
Reading	
Phone/Social Media	
TV/Series	
Listening to Music	
Creative Work	
Other: _____	
Other: _____	
Other: _____	

Body

	Type *Example: 15 push-ups*	Duration
Exercise		

- Shower: Yes ☐   No ☐
- Hair Wash: Yes ☐   No ☐
- Skincare Routine: Yes ☐   No ☐

Mood Tracker

Today I have felt...

☐   ☐   ☐   ☐   ☐

The Self-Care Journal
FOR TEENS

— REFLECTION —

❋ Gratitude

● Today I am grateful for _____

_____

_____

_____

● Best moments of the day:

_____

_____

_____

My notes / My thoughts

A POSITIVE AFFIRMATION

The Self-Care Journal
FOR TEENS

DAY 34

DATE: _____   Mo Tu We Th Fr Sa Su

— HABIT TRACKER —

Daily Basics

- SLEEP LOG | Duration: _____ Times: From _____ To _____
- CUPS OF WATER: _____
- HEALTHY EATING: Yes ☐   No ☐
- TIME OUTSIDE: _____

Mind

	Duration
○ Study	
○ Reading	
○ Phone/Social Media	
○ TV/Series	
○ Listening to Music	
○ Creative Work	
○ Other: _____	
○ Other: _____	
○ Other: _____	

Body

	Type	Duration
	Example: 15 push-ups	
● Exercise		

- Shower: Yes ☐ No ☐
- Hair Wash: Yes ☐ No ☐
- Skincare Routine: Yes ☐   No ☐

Mood Tracker

Today I have felt...

☺ ☺ 😐 ☹ 😕

☐ ☐ ☐ ☐ ☐

The Self-Care Journal
FOR TEENS

REFLECTION

❋ Gratitude

- Today I am grateful for _____

_____

_____

_____

- Best moments of the day:

_____

_____

_____

My notes/My thoughts

A POSITIVE AFFIRMATION

The Self-Care Journal
FOR TEENS

DAY 35

DATE: _____ Mo Tu We Th Fr Sa Su

— HABIT TRACKER —

Daily Basics

- SLEEP LOG | Duration: _____ Times: From _____ To _____
- CUPS OF WATER: _____
- HEALTHY EATING: Yes ☐   No ☐
- TIME OUTSIDE: _____

Mind

	Duration
Study	
Reading	
Phone/Social Media	
TV/Series	
Listening to Music	
Creative Work	
Other: _____	
Other: _____	
Other: _____	

Body

	Type	Duration
	Example: 15 push-ups	
Exercise		

- Shower: Yes ☐   No ☐
- Hair Wash: Yes ☐   No ☐
- Skincare Routine: Yes ☐   No ☐

Mood Tracker

Today I have felt...

☐   ☐   ☐   ☐   ☐

The Self-Care Journal
FOR TEENS

REFLECTION

❋ Gratitude

- Today I am grateful for _____

_____

_____

_____

- Best moments of the day:

_____

_____

_____

My notes / My thoughts

A POSITIVE AFFIRMATION

The Self-Care Journal
FOR TEENS

DAY 36

DATE: _____ Mo Tu We Th Fr Sa Su

— HABIT TRACKER —

✽ Daily Basics

- SLEEP LOG | Duration: _____ Times: From _____ To _____
- CUPS OF WATER: _____
- HEALTHY EATING: Yes ☐   No ☐
- TIME OUTSIDE: _____

Mind

	Duration
Study	
Reading	
Phone/Social Media	
TV/Series	
Listening to Music	
Creative Work	
Other: _____	
Other: _____	
Other: _____	

Body

	Type Example: 15 push-ups	Duration
Exercise		

- Shower: Yes ☐ No ☐
- Hair Wash: Yes ☐ No ☐
- Skincare Routine: Yes ☐   No ☐

Mood Tracker

Today I have felt...

☺ 🙂 😐 🙁 😠

☐   ☐   ☐   ☐   ☐

The Self-Care Journal
FOR TEENS

REFLECTION

🌸 Gratitude

● Today I am grateful for _____

_____

_____

_____

● Best moments of the day:

_____

_____

_____

My notes/My thoughts

A POSITIVE AFFIRMATION

The Self-Care Journal
FOR TEENS

DAY 37

DATE: _____   Mo Tu We Th Fr Sa Su

— HABIT TRACKER —

Daily Basics

- SLEEP LOG | Duration: _____ Times: From _____ To _____
- CUPS OF WATER: _____
- HEALTHY EATING: Yes ☐   No ☐
- TIME OUTSIDE: _____

Mind

	Duration
○ Study	
○ Reading	
○ Phone/Social Media	
○ TV/Series	
○ Listening to Music	
○ Creative Work	
○ Other: _____	
○ Other: _____	
○ Other: _____	

Body

	Type _Example: 15 push-ups_	Duration
● Exercise		

- ● Shower: Yes ☐ No ☐
- ● Hair Wash: Yes ☐ No ☐
- ● Skincare Routine: Yes ☐ No ☐

Mood Tracker

Today I have felt...

😀 😊 😐 🙁 😠
☐ ☐ ☐ ☐ ☐

The Self-Care Journal
FOR TEENS

— REFLECTION —

✿ Gratitude

● Today I am grateful for _____

_____

_____

_____

● Best moments of the day:

_____

_____

_____

My notes/My thoughts

A POSITIVE AFFIRMATION

The Self-Care Journal
FOR TEENS

DAY 38

DATE: _____   Mo Tu We Th Fr Sa Su

— HABIT TRACKER —

Daily Basics

- SLEEP LOG | Duration: _____ Times: From _____ To _____
- CUPS OF WATER: _____
- HEALTHY EATING: Yes ☐   No ☐
- TIME OUTSIDE: _____

Mind

	Duration
Study	
Reading	
Phone/Social Media	
TV/Series	
Listening to Music	
Creative Work	
Other: _____	
Other: _____	
Other: _____	

Body

	Type Example: 15 push-ups	Duration
Exercise		

- Shower: Yes ☐ No ☐
- Hair Wash: Yes ☐ No ☐
- Skincare Routine: Yes ☐ No ☐

Mood Tracker

Today I have felt...

☐   ☐   ☐   ☐   ☐

The Self-Care Journal
FOR TEENS

REFLECTION

✽ Gratitude

- Today I am grateful for _____

_____

_____

_____

- Best moments of the day:

_____

_____

_____

My notes/My thoughts

A POSITIVE AFFIRMATION

The Self-Care Journal
FOR TEENS

DAY 39

DATE: _____ Mo Tu We Th Fr Sa Su

— HABIT TRACKER —

Daily Basics
- SLEEP LOG | Duration: _____ Times: From _____ To _____
- CUPS OF WATER: _____
- HEALTHY EATING: Yes ☐ No ☐
- TIME OUTSIDE: _____

Mind

	Duration
Study	
Reading	
Phone/Social Media	
TV/Series	
Listening to Music	
Creative Work	
Other: _____	
Other: _____	
Other: _____	

Body

	Type _Example: 15 push-ups_	Duration
Exercise		

- Shower: Yes ☐ No ☐
- Hair Wash: Yes ☐ No ☐
- Skincare Routine: Yes ☐ No ☐

Mood Tracker

Today I have felt...

☐ ☐ ☐ ☐ ☐

The Self-Care Journal
FOR TEENS

REFLECTION

Gratitude

- Today I am grateful for _____

_____

_____

_____

- Best moments of the day:

_____

_____

_____

My notes/My thoughts

A POSITIVE AFFIRMATION

The Self-Care Journal
FOR TEENS

DAY 40

DATE: _____   Mo Tu We Th Fr Sa Su

— HABIT TRACKER —

Daily Basics

- SLEEP LOG | Duration: _____ Times: From _____ To _____
- CUPS OF WATER: _____
- HEALTHY EATING: Yes ☐   No ☐
- TIME OUTSIDE: _____

Mind

	Duration
Study	
Reading	
Phone/Social Media	
TV/Series	
Listening to Music	
Creative Work	
Other: _____	
Other: _____	
Other: _____	

Body

	Type	Duration
	Example: 15 push-ups	
Exercise		

- Shower: Yes ☐ No ☐
- Hair Wash: Yes ☐ No ☐
- Skincare Routine: Yes ☐ No ☐

Mood Tracker

Today I have felt...

☺ 🙂 😐 🙁 😣

☐ ☐ ☐ ☐ ☐

The Self-Care Journal
FOR TEENS

REFLECTION

🌸 Gratitude

- Today I am grateful for _____

_____

_____

_____

- Best moments of the day:

_____

_____

_____

My notes/My thoughts

A POSITIVE AFFIRMATION

The Self-Care Journal
FOR TEENS

DAY 41

DATE: _____   Mo Tu We Th Fr Sa Su

— HABIT TRACKER —

Daily Basics

- SLEEP LOG | Duration: _____ Times: From _____ To _____
- CUPS OF WATER: _____
- HEALTHY EATING: Yes ☐   No ☐
- TIME OUTSIDE: _____

Mind

	Duration
Study	
Reading	
Phone/Social Media	
TV/Series	
Listening to Music	
Creative Work	
Other: _____	
Other: _____	
Other: _____	

Body

	Type *Example: 15 push-ups*	Duration
Exercise		

- Shower: Yes ☐ No ☐
- Hair Wash: Yes ☐ No ☐
- Skincare Routine: Yes ☐ No ☐

Mood Tracker

Today I have felt...

☐ ☐ ☐ ☐ ☐

The Self-Care Journal
FOR TEENS

REFLECTION

❀ Gratitude

- Today I am grateful for _____

_____

_____

_____

- Best moments of the day:

_____

_____

_____

My notes/My thoughts

A POSITIVE AFFIRMATION

The Self-Care Journal
FOR TEENS

DAY 42

DATE:_____   Mo Tu We Th Fr Sa Su

— HABIT TRACKER —

Daily Basics

- SLEEP LOG | Duration: _____ Times: From _____ To _____
- CUPS OF WATER: _____
- HEALTHY EATING: Yes ☐   No ☐
- TIME OUTSIDE: _____

Mind

	Duration
Study	
Reading	
Phone/Social Media	
TV/Series	
Listening to Music	
Creative Work	
Other: _____	
Other: _____	
Other: _____	

Body

	Type	Duration
	Example: 15 push-ups	
Exercise		

- Shower: Yes ☐ No ☐
- Hair Wash: Yes ☐   No ☐
- Skincare Routine: Yes ☐   No ☐

Mood Tracker

Today I have felt...

☐   ☐   ☐   ☐   ☐

The Self-Care Journal
FOR TEENS

REFLECTION

🌸 Gratitude

- Today I am grateful for _____

_____

_____

_____

- Best moments of the day:

_____

_____

_____

My notes/My thoughts

A POSITIVE AFFIRMATION

The Self-Care Journal
FOR TEENS

DAY 43

DATE: _____   Mo Tu We Th Fr Sa Su

— HABIT TRACKER —

Daily Basics

- SLEEP LOG | Duration: _____ Times: From _____ To _____
- CUPS OF WATER: _____
- HEALTHY EATING: Yes ☐   No ☐
- TIME OUTSIDE: _____

Mind

	Duration
○ Study	
○ Reading	
○ Phone/Social Media	
○ TV/Series	
○ Listening to Music	
○ Creative Work	
○ Other: _____	
○ Other: _____	
○ Other: _____	

Body

	Type Example: 15 push-ups	Duration
● Exercise		

- ● Shower: Yes ☐ No ☐
- ● Hair Wash: Yes ☐ No ☐
- ● Skincare Routine: Yes ☐ No ☐

Mood Tracker

Today I have felt...

😃 🙂 😐 🙁 😣

☐ ☐ ☐ ☐ ☐

The Self-Care Journal
FOR TEENS

REFLECTION

❀ Gratitude

● Today I am grateful for _____

_____

_____

_____

● Best moments of the day:

_____

_____

_____

My notes/My thoughts

A POSITIVE AFFIRMATION

The Self-Care Journal
FOR TEENS

DAY 44

DATE:_____   Mo Tu We Th Fr Sa Su

— HABIT TRACKER —

❀ Daily Basics

- SLEEP LOG | Duration: _____ Times: From _____ To _____
- CUPS OF WATER: _____
- HEALTHY EATING: Yes ☐   No ☐
- TIME OUTSIDE: _____

Mind

	Duration
Study	
Reading	
Phone/Social Media	
TV/Series	
Listening to Music	
Creative Work	
Other: _____	
Other: _____	
Other: _____	

Body

	Type Example: 15 push-ups	Duration
Exercise		

- Shower: Yes ☐ No ☐
- Hair Wash: Yes ☐   No ☐
- Skincare Routine: Yes ☐   No ☐

Mood Tracker

Today I have felt...

☐   ☐   ☐   ☐   ☐

The Self-Care Journal
FOR TEENS

REFLECTION

❀ Gratitude

- Today I am grateful for _____

_____

_____

_____

- Best moments of the day:

_____

_____

_____

My notes/My thoughts

A POSITIVE AFFIRMATION

The Self-Care Journal
FOR TEENS

DAY 45

DATE: _____   Mo Tu We Th Fr Sa Su

— HABIT TRACKER —

Daily Basics

- SLEEP LOG | Duration: _____ Times: From _____ To _____
- CUPS OF WATER: _____
- HEALTHY EATING: Yes ☐   No ☐
- TIME OUTSIDE: _____

Mind

	Duration
○ Study	
○ Reading	
○ Phone/Social Media	
○ TV/Series	
○ Listening to Music	
○ Creative Work	
○ Other: _____	
○ Other: _____	
○ Other: _____	

Body

	Type _Example: 15 push-ups_	Duration
● Exercise		

- Shower: Yes ☐ No ☐
- Hair Wash: Yes ☐ No ☐
- Skincare Routine: Yes ☐ No ☐

Mood Tracker

Today I have felt...

☐ ☐ ☐ ☐ ☐

The Self-Care Journal
FOR TEENS

REFLECTION

Gratitude

● Today I am grateful for _____

_____

_____

_____

● Best moments of the day:

_____

_____

_____

My notes/My thoughts

A POSITIVE AFFIRMATION

The Self-Care Journal
FOR TEENS

DAY 46

DATE: _____   Mo Tu We Th Fr Sa Su

— HABIT TRACKER —

Daily Basics

- SLEEP LOG | Duration: _____ Times: From _____ To _____
- CUPS OF WATER: _____
- HEALTHY EATING: Yes ☐   No ☐
- TIME OUTSIDE: _____

Mind

	Duration
Study	
Reading	
Phone/Social Media	
TV/Series	
Listening to Music	
Creative Work	
Other: _____	
Other: _____	
Other: _____	

Body

	Type Example: 15 push-ups	Duration
Exercise		

- Shower: Yes ☐   No ☐
- Hair Wash: Yes ☐   No ☐
- Skincare Routine: Yes ☐   No ☐

Mood Tracker

Today I have felt...

☐   ☐   ☐   ☐   ☐

The Self-Care Journal
FOR TEENS

— REFLECTION —

❋ Gratitude

● Today I am grateful for _____

_____

_____

_____

● Best moments of the day:

_____

_____

_____

My notes/My thoughts

A POSITIVE AFFIRMATION

The Self-Care Journal
FOR TEENS

DAY 47

DATE: _____   Mo Tu We Th Fr Sa Su

— HABIT TRACKER —

✿ Daily Basics

- SLEEP LOG | Duration: _____ Times: From _____ To _____
- CUPS OF WATER: _____
- HEALTHY EATING: Yes ☐   No ☐
- TIME OUTSIDE: _____

Mind

	Duration
○ Study	
○ Reading	
○ Phone/Social Media	
○ TV/Series	
○ Listening to Music	
○ Creative Work	
○ Other: _____	
○ Other: _____	
○ Other: _____	

Body

	Type *Example: 15 push-ups*	Duration
● Exercise		

- ● Shower: Yes ☐ No ☐
- ● Hair Wash: Yes ☐ No ☐
- ● Skincare Routine: Yes ☐ No ☐

Mood Tracker

Today I have felt...

☐   ☐   ☐   ☐   ☐

The Self-Care Journal
FOR TEENS

REFLECTION

✿ Gratitude

● Today I am grateful for _____

_____

_____

_____

● Best moments of the day:

_____

_____

_____

My notes/My thoughts

A POSITIVE AFFIRMATION

The Self-Care Journal
FOR TEENS

DAY 48

DATE: _____   Mo Tu We Th Fr Sa Su

— HABIT TRACKER —

Daily Basics

- SLEEP LOG | Duration: _____ Times: From _____ To _____
- CUPS OF WATER: _____
- HEALTHY EATING: Yes ☐   No ☐
- TIME OUTSIDE: _____

Mind

	Duration
○ Study	
○ Reading	
○ Phone/Social Media	
○ TV/Series	
○ Listening to Music	
○ Creative Work	
○ Other: _____	
○ Other: _____	
○ Other: _____	

Body

	Type (Example: 15 push-ups)	Duration
● Exercise		

- Shower: Yes ☐ No ☐
- Hair Wash: Yes ☐ No ☐
- Skincare Routine: Yes ☐ No ☐

Mood Tracker

Today I have felt...

☐ ☐ ☐ ☐ ☐

The Self-Care Journal
FOR TEENS

REFLECTION

❀ Gratitude

● Today I am grateful for _____

_____

_____

_____

● Best moments of the day:

_____

_____

_____

My notes/My thoughts

A POSITIVE AFFIRMATION

The Self-Care Journal
FOR TEENS

DAY 49

DATE: _____   Mo Tu We Th Fr Sa Su

— HABIT TRACKER —

❋ Daily Basics

- SLEEP LOG | Duration: _____ Times: From _____ To _____
- CUPS OF WATER: _____
- HEALTHY EATING: Yes ☐   No ☐
- TIME OUTSIDE: _____

Mind

	Duration
Study	
Reading	
Phone/Social Media	
TV/Series	
Listening to Music	
Creative Work	
Other: _____	
Other: _____	
Other: _____	

Body

	Type	Duration
	Example: 15 push-ups	
Exercise		

- Shower: Yes ☐   No ☐
- Hair Wash: Yes ☐   No ☐
- Skincare Routine: Yes ☐   No ☐

Mood Tracker

Today I have felt...

😀 🙂 😐 ☹️ 😣

☐   ☐   ☐   ☐   ☐

The Self-Care Journal
FOR TEENS

— REFLECTION —

❀ Gratitude

● Today I am grateful for _____

_____

_____

_____

● Best moments of the day:

_____

_____

_____

My notes/My thoughts

A POSITIVE AFFIRMATION

The Self-Care Journal
FOR TEENS

DAY 50

DATE: _____   Mo Tu We Th Fr Sa Su

— HABIT TRACKER —

Daily Basics

- SLEEP LOG | Duration: _____ Times: From _____ To _____
- CUPS OF WATER: _____
- HEALTHY EATING: Yes ☐   No ☐
- TIME OUTSIDE: _____

Mind

	Duration
Study	
Reading	
Phone/Social Media	
TV/Series	
Listening to Music	
Creative Work	
Other: _____	
Other: _____	
Other: _____	

Body

	Type _Example: 15 push-ups_	Duration
Exercise		

- Shower: Yes ☐ No ☐
- Hair Wash: Yes ☐ No ☐
- Skincare Routine: Yes ☐ No ☐

Mood Tracker

Today I have felt...

☐   ☐   ☐   ☐   ☐

The Self-Care Journal
FOR TEENS

REFLECTION

❃ Gratitude

- Today I am grateful for _____

_____

_____

_____

- Best moments of the day:

_____

_____

_____

My notes/My thoughts

A POSITIVE AFFIRMATION

The Self-Care Journal
FOR TEENS

DAY 51

DATE: _____   Mo Tu We Th Fr Sa Su

— HABIT TRACKER —

Daily Basics

- SLEEP LOG | Duration: _____ Times: From _____ To _____
- CUPS OF WATER: _____
- HEALTHY EATING: Yes ☐   No ☐
- TIME OUTSIDE: _____

Mind

	Duration
Study	
Reading	
Phone/Social Media	
TV/Series	
Listening to Music	
Creative Work	
Other: _____	
Other: _____	
Other: _____	

Body

	Type _Example: 15 push-ups_	Duration
Exercise		

- Shower: Yes ☐ No ☐
- Hair Wash: Yes ☐ No ☐
- Skincare Routine: Yes ☐ No ☐

Mood Tracker

Today I have felt...

☐ ☐ ☐ ☐ ☐

The Self-Care Journal
FOR TEENS

REFLECTION

❀ Gratitude

- Today I am grateful for _____

_____

_____

_____

- Best moments of the day:

_____

_____

_____

My notes/My thoughts

A POSITIVE AFFIRMATION

The Self-Care Journal
FOR TEENS

DAY 52

DATE: _____   Mo Tu We Th Fr Sa Su

— HABIT TRACKER —

❁ Daily Basics

- SLEEP LOG | Duration: _____ Times: From _____ To _____
- CUPS OF WATER: _____
- HEALTHY EATING: Yes ☐   No ☐
- TIME OUTSIDE: _____

Mind

	Duration
Study	
Reading	
Phone/Social Media	
TV/Series	
Listening to Music	
Creative Work	
Other: _____	
Other: _____	
Other: _____	

Body

	Type *Example: 15 push-ups*	Duration
Exercise		

- Shower: Yes ☐ No ☐
- Hair Wash: Yes ☐ No ☐
- Skincare Routine: Yes ☐ No ☐

Mood Tracker

Today I have felt...

☐   ☐   ☐   ☐   ☐

The Self-Care Journal
FOR TEENS

REFLECTION

✿ Gratitude

● Today I am grateful for _____

_____

_____

_____

● Best moments of the day:

_____

_____

_____

My notes/My thoughts

A POSITIVE AFFIRMATION

The Self-Care Journal
FOR TEENS

DAY 53

DATE: _____   Mo Tu We Th Fr Sa Su

— HABIT TRACKER —

Daily Basics

- SLEEP LOG | Duration: _____ Times: From _____ To _____
- CUPS OF WATER: _____
- HEALTHY EATING: Yes ☐   No ☐
- TIME OUTSIDE: _____

Mind

	Duration
Study	
Reading	
Phone/Social Media	
TV/Series	
Listening to Music	
Creative Work	
Other: _____	
Other: _____	
Other: _____	

Body

	Type Example: 15 push-ups	Duration
Exercise		

- Shower: Yes ☐   No ☐
- Hair Wash: Yes ☐   No ☐
- Skincare Routine: Yes ☐   No ☐

Mood Tracker

Today I have felt...

☐   ☐   ☐   ☐   ☐

The Self-Care Journal
FOR TEENS

REFLECTION

Gratitude

● Today I am grateful for _____

_____

_____

_____

● Best moments of the day:

_____

_____

_____

My notes/My thoughts

A POSITIVE AFFIRMATION

The Self-Care Journal
FOR TEENS

DAY 54

DATE: _____   Mo Tu We Th Fr Sa Su

— HABIT TRACKER —

Daily Basics

- SLEEP LOG | Duration: _____ Times: From _____ To _____
- CUPS OF WATER: _____
- HEALTHY EATING: Yes ☐   No ☐
- TIME OUTSIDE: _____

Mind

	Duration
Study	
Reading	
Phone/Social Media	
TV/Series	
Listening to Music	
Creative Work	
Other: _____	
Other: _____	
Other: _____	

Body

	Type Example: 15 push-ups	Duration
Exercise		

- Shower: Yes ☐ No ☐
- Hair Wash: Yes ☐ No ☐
- Skincare Routine: Yes ☐ No ☐

Mood Tracker

Today I have felt...

☐   ☐   ☐   ☐   ☐

The Self-Care Journal
FOR TEENS

— REFLECTION —

❋ Gratitude

● Today I am grateful for _____

_____

_____

_____

● Best moments of the day:

_____

_____

_____

My notes/My thoughts

A POSITIVE AFFIRMATION

The Self-Care Journal
FOR TEENS

DAY 55

DATE: _____ Mo Tu We Th Fr Sa Su

— HABIT TRACKER —

Daily Basics

- SLEEP LOG | Duration: _____ Times: From _____ To _____
- CUPS OF WATER: _____
- HEALTHY EATING: Yes ☐   No ☐
- TIME OUTSIDE: _____

Mind

	Duration
Study	
Reading	
Phone/Social Media	
TV/Series	
Listening to Music	
Creative Work	
Other: _____	
Other: _____	
Other: _____	

Body

	Type	Duration
Exercise	*Example: 15 push-ups*	

- Shower: Yes ☐ No ☐
- Hair Wash: Yes ☐   No ☐
- Skincare Routine: Yes ☐   No ☐

Mood Tracker

Today I have felt...

☐ ☐ ☐ ☐ ☐

The Self-Care Journal
FOR TEENS

REFLECTION

✿ Gratitude

● Today I am grateful for _____

_____

_____

_____

● Best moments of the day:

_____

_____

_____

My notes / My thoughts

A POSITIVE AFFIRMATION

The Self-Care Journal
FOR TEENS

DAY 56

DATE: _____ Mo Tu We Th Fr Sa Su

— HABIT TRACKER —

❋ Daily Basics

- SLEEP LOG | Duration: _____ Times: From _____ To _____
- CUPS OF WATER: _____
- HEALTHY EATING: Yes ☐   No ☐
- TIME OUTSIDE: _____

Mind

	Duration
Study	
Reading	
Phone/Social Media	
TV/Series	
Listening to Music	
Creative Work	
Other: _____	
Other: _____	
Other: _____	

Body

	Type Example: 15 push-ups	Duration
Exercise		

- Shower: Yes ☐ No ☐
- Hair Wash: Yes ☐ No ☐
- Skincare Routine: Yes ☐ No ☐

Mood Tracker

Today I have felt...

☐ ☐ ☐ ☐ ☐

The Self-Care Journal
FOR TEENS

REFLECTION

✿ Gratitude

● Today I am grateful for _____

_____

_____

_____

● Best moments of the day:

_____

_____

_____

My notes/My thoughts

A POSITIVE AFFIRMATION

The Self-Care Journal
FOR TEENS

DAY 57

DATE: _____ Mo Tu We Th Fr Sa Su

— HABIT TRACKER —

Daily Basics

- SLEEP LOG | Duration: _____ Times: From _____ To _____
- CUPS OF WATER: _____
- HEALTHY EATING: Yes ☐   No ☐
- TIME OUTSIDE: _____

Mind

	Duration
○ Study	
○ Reading	
○ Phone/Social Media	
○ TV/Series	
○ Listening to Music	
○ Creative Work	
○ Other: _____	
○ Other: _____	
○ Other: _____	

Body

	Type Example: 15 push-ups	Duration
● Exercise		

- ● Shower: Yes ☐ No ☐
- ● Hair Wash: Yes ☐ No ☐
- ● Skincare Routine: Yes ☐ No ☐

Mood Tracker

Today I have felt...

☺ 🙂 😐 🙁 😠

☐ ☐ ☐ ☐ ☐

The Self-Care Journal
FOR TEENS

REFLECTION

Gratitude

● Today I am grateful for _____

_____

_____

_____

● Best moments of the day:

_____

_____

_____

My notes/My thoughts

A POSITIVE AFFIRMATION

The Self-Care Journal
FOR TEENS

DAY 58

DATE: _____   Mo Tu We Th Fr Sa Su

— HABIT TRACKER —

Daily Basics

- SLEEP LOG | Duration: _____ Times: From _____ To _____
- CUPS OF WATER: _____
- HEALTHY EATING: Yes ☐   No ☐
- TIME OUTSIDE: _____

Mind

	Duration
Study	
Reading	
Phone/Social Media	
TV/Series	
Listening to Music	
Creative Work	
Other: _____	
Other: _____	
Other: _____	

Body

	Type Example: 15 push-ups	Duration
Exercise		

- Shower: Yes ☐ No ☐
- Hair Wash: Yes ☐   No ☐
- Skincare Routine: Yes ☐   No ☐

Mood Tracker

Today I have felt...

☐   ☐   ☐   ☐   ☐

The Self-Care Journal
FOR TEENS

DAY 58

REFLECTION

Gratitude

- Today I am grateful for _____

_____

_____

_____

- Best moments of the day:

_____

_____

_____

My notes/My thoughts

A POSITIVE AFFIRMATION

The Self-Care Journal
FOR TEENS

DAY 59

DATE: _____ Mo Tu We Th Fr Sa Su

— HABIT TRACKER —

Daily Basics

- SLEEP LOG | Duration: _____ Times: From _____ To _____
- CUPS OF WATER: _____
- HEALTHY EATING: Yes ☐   No ☐
- TIME OUTSIDE: _____

Mind

	Duration
Study	
Reading	
Phone/Social Media	
TV/Series	
Listening to Music	
Creative Work	
Other: _____	
Other: _____	
Other: _____	

Body

	Type	Duration
	Example: 15 push-ups	
Exercise		

- Shower: Yes ☐ No ☐
- Hair Wash: Yes ☐ No ☐
- Skincare Routine: Yes ☐ No ☐

Mood Tracker

Today I have felt...

☐   ☐   ☐   ☐   ☐

The Self-Care Journal
FOR TEENS

REFLECTION

✿ Gratitude

● Today I am grateful for _____

_____

_____

_____

● Best moments of the day:

_____

_____

_____

My notes/My thoughts

A POSITIVE AFFIRMATION

The Self-Care Journal
FOR TEENS

DAY 60

DATE: _____   Mo Tu We Th Fr Sa Su

— HABIT TRACKER —

❀ Daily Basics

- SLEEP LOG | Duration: _____ Times: From _____ To _____
- CUPS OF WATER: _____
- HEALTHY EATING: Yes ☐   No ☐
- TIME OUTSIDE: _____

Mind

	Duration
Study	
Reading	
Phone/Social Media	
TV/Series	
Listening to Music	
Creative Work	
Other: _____	
Other: _____	
Other: _____	

Body

Type Example: 15 push-ups	Duration
Exercise	

- Shower: Yes ☐ No ☐
- Hair Wash: Yes ☐ No ☐
- Skincare Routine: Yes ☐ No ☐

Mood Tracker

Today I have felt...

😀 🙂 😐 🙁 😕

☐ ☐ ☐ ☐ ☐

The Self-Care Journal
FOR TEENS

— REFLECTION —

🌸 Gratitude

● Today I am grateful for _____

_____

_____

_____

● Best moments of the day:

_____

_____

_____

My notes/My thoughts

A POSITIVE AFFIRMATION

Thank you,
thank you,
thank you
for your purchase!

If you enjoyed and found useful The Self-Care
Journal for Teens, you would help me a lot
writing a positive review on Amazon

Made in the USA
Columbia, SC
21 March 2025

55475965R00070